Louisiana
The Pelican State

Miriam Coleman

PowerKiDS press™

New York

Published in 2011 by The Rosen Publishing Group, Inc.
29 East 21st Street, New York, NY 10010

First Edition

Editor: Joanne Randolph
Book Design: Greg Tucker
Layout Design: Kate Laczynski
Photo Researcher: Jessica Gerweck

Photo Credits: Cover, pp. 11, 13, 15, 17, 22 (bird, flower) Shutterstock.com; p. 5 © Felix Stenson/age fotostock; p. 7 MPI/Getty Images; p. 9 © Wojtek Buss/age fotostock; p. 19 Cosma Condina/Getty Images; p. 22 (tree, dog) Wikimedia Commons; p. 22 (Louis Armstrong) Gilles Petard/Getty Images; p. 22 (Truman Capote) John Downing/Espress/Getty Images; p. 22 (Kordell Stewart) Sam Greenwood/ Getty Images.

Library of Congress Cataloging-in-Publication Data

Coleman, Miriam.
    Louisiana : the Pelican State / Miriam Coleman. — 1st ed.
        p. cm. — (Our amazing states)
    Includes index.
    ISBN 978-1-4488-0654-6 (library binding) — ISBN 978-1-4488-0740-6 (pbk.) —
ISBN 978-1-4488-0741-3 (6-pack)
    1. Louisiana—Juvenile literature. I. Title.
    F369.3.C65 2011
    976.3—dc22
                                    2009048546

Manufactured in the United States of America

CPSIA Compliance Information: Batch #WS10PK: For Further Information contact Rosen Publishing, New York, New York at 1-800-237-9932

Contents

A State Like No Other

Louisiana is like no other place on Earth. Found in the far south of the United States, Louisiana has a rich and **unique culture** that draws from the French, Spanish, African, and Caribbean people who have lived there. Many people in Louisiana even speak French, including two **dialects** called Cajun and Creole French.

The northern part of Louisiana is a land of rolling hills and forests of pine trees. The southern part of the state is crisscrossed with rivers, **creeks**, and **marshes**. Louisiana is **divided** into 64 different counties, which are called parishes. This name comes from the time of Spanish rule, when the **Catholic** Church helped govern the land.

4

Riding on a paddle steamer is a way for visitors to see sights along the Mississippi River. This one has docked at the port in New Orleans, Louisiana.

STEAMER

PORT OF NEW ORLEANS

The Louisiana Purchase

Native American groups who built their villages around large earthen mounds were the first people to settle Louisiana. The first European **explorers** were the Spanish who came in 1541. French explorer René-Robert Cavelier de la Salle arrived in the 1680s and claimed the land along the Mississippi River for France. He named it after the French king Louis XIV.

Over the next hundred years, rule of Louisiana **shifted** to Britain and Spain and then back to France. In 1803, the United States, led by President Thomas Jefferson, bought the land from France for $15 million. The land included in the Louisiana Purchase reached from the Gulf of Mexico all the way up to Canada. It would later be divided into 15 different states. Louisiana became a state on April 30, 1812.

U.S. statesmen James Monroe and Robert Livingston meet with French statesman Charles-Maurice de Talleyrand-Périgord about the Louisiana Territory (see map inset).

THE LOUISIANA PURCHASE.
MESSRS. MONROE AND LIVINGSTONE COMPLETING NEGOTIATIONS WITH TALLYRAND, APRIL 30, 1803

COPYRIG

So Many Rivers

Louisiana is shaped like a boot, with a ragged toe that sticks out into the Gulf of Mexico. Many rivers, including the Mississippi and the Atchafalaya, flow through Louisiana and into the gulf. Because of all these rivers, much of the land in the state is covered in marshes and **swamps**.

Louisiana's weather is hot and wet, with lots of rain. The state often sees terrible storms and even **hurricanes**. Hurricane Katrina, one of the worst storms in American history, hit Louisiana and its neighbors in August 2005. Lakes and rivers overflowed in the storm waters and floods covered many cities. New Orleans had a lot of flooding during the storm. Many people had to leave. The city continues to clean up and rebuild years later.

This is a bayou near Lafitte, Louisiana. Lafitte has an area of 7.8 square miles (20 sq km) and around 2 square miles (5 sq km) of this is covered in water.

Jambalaya on the Bayou

A bayou is a slow-moving body of water that flows from a larger river or lake. Louisiana's bayous are an important part of its landscape. The bayous are home to many shrimp, crawfish, catfish, and alligators that end up on Louisiana dinner plates!

Many of Louisiana's bayous lie in a part of southern Louisiana that people call Cajun country. Cajuns are **descendants** of French settlers who came to Louisiana from a part of Canada called Acadia. They first settled around Bayou Lafourche and Bayou Teche in the 1760s. Cajuns are famous for their cooking, which includes blackened fish and jambalaya, a spicy dish of rice with sausage and other meat. Cajun music, which has accordions, guitars, and fiddles, is also popular.

This is a cabin on the banks of a Louisiana bayou. Most of the bayous are in the southern part of the state, where the rivers slow down and spread out before emptying into the sea.

Wild Louisiana!

Louisiana's forests, marshes, and swamps are home to many different kinds of plant and animal life. Trees like magnolias, oaks, bald cypresses, and longleaf pines grow in forests. Spanish moss hangs from many of the trees. The blossoms from the magnolia tree are Louisiana's state flower. Other flowers like honeysuckle, jasmine, orchids, and lilies grow all over the state.

Raccoons, skunks, and wild hogs live in Louisiana's forests. Alligators live in the marshes and bayous. Louisiana gets its nickname from its state bird, the brown pelican. This bird lives in marshes near the coast. Pelicans are large seabirds with special pockets under their bills, which they use to catch fish.

This is a brown pelican. Its wings are about 78 inches (200 cm) from tip to tip. It is the only pelican that dives from the air to catch fish.

Sugar, Salt, and Shipping

   Louisiana lies between the sea and the Mississippi River, which flows all the way up to Minnesota. This makes it a great place for shipping since boats and goods can come from all over the world and sail up the river. New Orleans has one of the busiest ports in the world. Baton Rouge has a big port, too.

   Food is another big business in Louisiana. Shrimp, crab, catfish, crawfish, and oysters come out of the state's huge fishing trade. Salt comes from mines near the coast and sugarcane grows on farms. Louisiana is also famous for making Tabasco sauce. People all over the world use this spicy, red hot sauce.

This cargo ship carries goods to New Orleans. More than 6,000 ships travel through New Orleans each year to carry cargo up the Mississippi River.

Head on Down to Baton Rouge

Baton Rouge was named Louisiana's capital in 1849. Baton Rouge sits alongside the Mississippi River, in the southeast part of the state. The city's name means "red stick" in French. The name came from an early French explorer, who noted on his map a red cypress pole that marked the hunting grounds of two Native American tribes.

Baton Rouge is home to Louisiana State University and Southern University. For those interested in the arts, the River Center hosts dance, theater, and other live performances. The Shaw Center is another great place to see some art, catch a show, or to grab a bite to eat. The Louisiana Art and Science **Museum** and the Baton Rouge Zoo are favorite stops for kids, as well.

The Louisiana State Capitol, where the state government meets, is 34 stories high. This makes it the tallest state capitol in the country!

A Trip to the Crescent City

New Orleans is likely Louisiana's best-known city. People call it the **Crescent** City because it lies on a crescent-shaped bend in the Mississippi River. French Canadians founded the city in 1718. Parts of the city, such as the French Quarter, still feel like a bit of France. New Orleans is also famous for its beautiful gardens, delicious food, and its jazz music. There are plenty of art, children's, and history museums in New Orleans, too.

Every year, people from all over the world head to New Orleans for Mardi Gras, a celebration that begins in January and ends in February. People fill the streets for the carnival, with its wild parades, costumes, and music.

Here a marching band plays in a parade through New Orleans's French Quarter. Many people visit the French Quarter each year.

Visiting the Pelican State

Louisiana's special blend of cultures has created some of the best food and music in the world. Millions of people come to **experience** it for themselves. They listen to the Cajun, jazz, and zydeco music that fills the city streets and drifts across the bayous. If history is your interest, there are museums throughout the state about African-American heritage, the Louisiana Purchase, the Civil War, and more.

From quiet marshes and grand old **plantations** to colorful, bustling cities, Louisiana has so many places to discover. There are also lots of friendly people to show you the way.

Glossary

Catholic (KATH-lik) Of the Roman Catholic faith.

creeks (KREEKS) Small streams.

crescent (KREH-sent) Something that is shaped like a curved moon.

culture (KUL-chur) The beliefs, practices, and arts of a group of people.

descendants (dih-SEN-dents) People who are born of a certain family or group.

dialects (DY-uh-lekts) Different ways that a language is spoken in different areas.

divided (dih-VYD-ed) Broken apart or separated.

experience (ik-SPEER-ee-ents) To learn by taking part or seeing for oneself.

explorers (ek-SPLOR-erz) People who travel and look for new land.

hurricanes (HUR-ih-kaynz) Storms with strong winds and heavy rains.

marshes (MAHRSH-ez) Areas of soft, wet land.

museum (myoo-ZEE-um) A place where art or historical pieces are safely kept for people to see and to study.

plantations (plan-TAY-shunz) Very large farms where crops are grown.

shifted (SHIFT-ed) Moved from one thing to another.

swamps (SWOMPS) Wet lands with a lot of trees and bushes.

unique (yoo-NEEK) One of a kind.

Louisiana State Symbols

State Tree
Bald Cypress

State Dog
Catahoula
Leopard Dog

State Flag

State Bird
Eastern Brown
Pelican

State Flower
Magnolia

State Seal

Famous People from Louisiana

Louis Armstrong
(1901–1971)
Born in New Orleans, LA
Musician

Truman Capote
(1924–1984)
Born in New Orleans, LA
Writer

Kordell Stewart
(1972–)
Born in New Orleans, LA
NFL Quarterback

Louisiana State Map

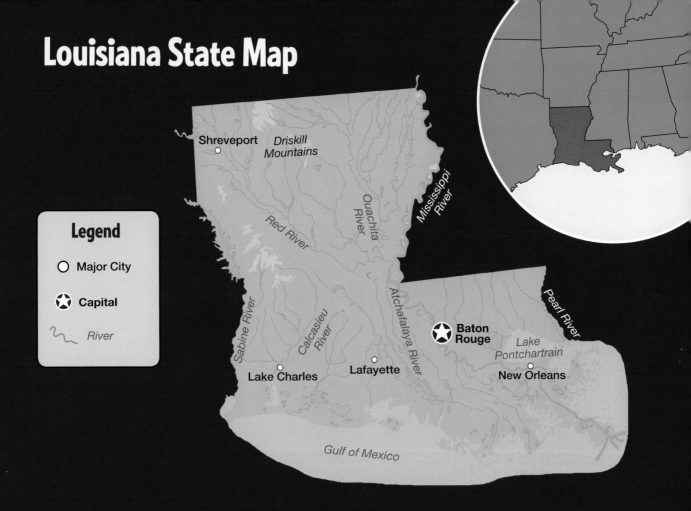

Legend

○ Major City

★ Capital

〰 River

Shreveport
Driskill Mountains
Ouachita River
Mississippi River
Red River
Sabine River
Calcasieu River
Atchafalaya River
Baton Rouge
Pearl River
Lake Pontchartrain
Lake Charles
Lafayette
New Orleans
Gulf of Mexico

Louisiana State Facts

Population: About 4,468,976

Area: 47,717 square miles (123,586 sq km)

Motto: Union, Justice, and Confidence

Songs: "Give Me Louisiana" and "You Are My Sunshine"

Index

Web Sites

Due to the changing nature of Internet links, PowerKids Press has developed an online list of Web sites related to the subject of this book. This site is updated regularly. Please use this link to access the list:
www.powerkidslinks.com/amst/la/